BOO

CW00434674

The Murder of Roger Ackroyd

BY AGATHA CHRISTIE

Bright
≡Summaries.com

BOOK ANALYSIS

**Shed new light
on your favorite books with**

Bright
≡Summaries.com

www.brightsummaries.com

AGATHA CHRISTIE

ENGLISH NOVELIST

- **Born in Torquay, Devon in 1890.**
- **Died in Wallingford, Oxfordshire in 1976.**
- **Notable works:**
  - *Murder on the Orient Express* (1934), novel
  - *The ABC Murders* (1936), novel
  - *And Then There Were None* (1939), novel

Known for her murder mysteries, Agatha Christie is the best-selling novelist of all time. She has written a total of 66 detective novels, along with 14 collections of short stories and several plays, including *The Mousetrap*, which is the world's longest running play. Over a billion copies of her works have been sold in English alone. Christie is viewed as the creator of the traditional detective novel, introducing many of the tropes now associated with the genre. She is best-known for her works featuring the characters of Hercule Poirot and Miss Marple. Christie has been given numerous awards for her writings and was the first ever recipient of the Mystery Writers of

America's highest honour, the Grand Master Award. In 1971, she was awarded a DBE for her contributions to literature.

Christie married twice and had one daughter, Rosalind, in 1919. Christie participated in the war effort in both the First and the Second World Wars, working in hospital dispensaries, where she acquired much of her knowledge of poisons. Christie's family continue to manage her estate to this day, with her great-grandson now the chair of Agatha Christie Ltd.

THE MURDER OF ROGER ACKROYD

ONE OF THE GREATEST TWISTS OF ALL TIME

- **Genre:** novel
- **Reference edition:** Christie, A. (1957) *The Murder of Roger Ackroyd*. London: Fontana.
- **1st edition:** 1926
- **Themes:** mystery, thriller, secrecy, deception, gossip, wealth

The Murder of Roger Ackroyd was the third of Christie's novels to feature Hercule Poirot, a peculiar Belgian detective with a talent for solving difficult cases using his "little grey cells". In this novel, Poirot is pulled out of retirement to investigate the murder of his wealthy industrialist friend. The tale of blackmail and murder is known for its surprising ending, often heralded as one of the best twists of all time.

In 2013, the British Crime Writers' Association voted *The Murder of Roger Ackroyd* the best crime novel ever written. It was the first of Christie's works to be published by HarperCollins and the first to be adapted for the stage. The novel remains one of Christie's best-known works, and is one of her most controversial, with some criticising her breaches of the conventions of detective fiction.

SUMMARY

WELCOME TO KING'S ABBOT

The novel is narrated by Dr James Sheppard, who lives with his nosy sister Caroline in the village of King's Abbot. The village is quiet and traditional and contains two large houses, one owned by the widow Mrs Ferrars, whose husband died a year previously, and the other by Roger Ackroyd, a widower who lives with his stepson Ralph, his sister-in-law, her daughter Flora, and his housekeeper Miss Russell. The novel opens with the death of Mrs Ferrars: Caroline believes that she killed herself out of guilt because she poisoned her husband. Roger Ackroyd, with whom Sheppard is friendly, invites Sheppard to dinner that night. Miss Russell later visits his surgery and asks about drug addiction and poisons. Sheppard meets his new neighbour, a retired 'Mr Porrot', and visits Ralph, who tells him that he is staying at an inn after a row with his stepfather.

Sheppard arrives at Roger Ackroyd's house at half past seven and dines with Roger, Mrs Ackroyd,

Flora, Geoffrey Raymond (Roger's secretary) and Major Hector Blunt (Roger's friend). After dinner, Roger takes Sheppard to his office and reveals that Mrs Ferrars, with whom he was romantically involved, did indeed kill her husband and was being blackmailed. Roger receives a letter from Mrs Ferrars revealing the identity of the blackmailer and asks Sheppard to leave while he reads it. Sheppard leaves, encountering a familiar stranger on his way out. In the night Sheppard receives a phone call telling him that Roger has been murdered. He returns to the house, where the butler Parker denies making the call. However, Roger is found stabbed in the study and the police are called. Raymond heard Roger talking to someone at half past nine. Flora seems to have been the last to see Roger alive, saying goodnight to him at 10pm.

The letter has vanished, so Sheppard tells the police about the blackmail. They learn that Roger was stabbed with his own ornate knife. Sheppard had heard someone looking in the silver box, where the knife was kept, when he arrived for dinner.

POIROT JOINS THE INVESTIGATION

Sheppard discovers that Ralph has left the inn but keeps the information to himself. Flora, who is engaged to Ralph, fears that he will be a suspect, so she reveals Poirot's identity and asks him to investigate. Poirot asks Sheppard to assist him. Poirot examines the scene and learns that Parker, the chief suspect, has been cleared by fingerprints. Parker reveals that a chair has been moved in the study and the police find footprints on the windowsill matching Ralph's shoes. The police focus their attention on Ralph while Poirot and Sheppard examine the garden, finding a scrap of fabric and a quill in the summerhouse. Poirot and Sheppard overhear a conversation between Blunt and Flora, in which Blunt appears interested in her. They then find a wedding ring in the pond with an 'R' inscribed on it.

Roger's will is read: Flora, Miss Russell, Raymond and Mrs Ackroyd have all inherited, but Ralph has received the most. Raymond discovers that £40 is missing from Roger's desk, leading to Poirot questioning the maids. One, Ursula Bourne, was fired that day for touching papers in Roger's office and has no alibi. Poirot sends Sheppard to talk to Ursula's former employer, who refuses to talk. Poirot talks with Caroline and learns from her that Miss Russell visited Sheppard and that Ralph had been meeting a mystery girl in the woods. The inquest is held, and Poirot tells the police that the fingerprints on the knife are the victim's own. He assembles everyone - Blunt, Flora, Mrs Ackroyd, Raymond, and Sheppard - together and accuses everybody of concealing something.

THE CONFESSIONS BEGIN

Poirot and Sheppard dine together and Sheppard worries that Ralph may be guilty. Poirot, however, believes he is innocent. Poirot deduces that the stranger visiting the house was Canadian and was meeting someone in the summerhouse, not Roger in his office. Mrs Ackroyd confesses to Sheppard that she was the one who looked through Roger's papers, hoping to find his will, and that she left the silver box open. Poirot wonders why Ursula would falsely confess to moving the papers and wants to know the colour of Ralph's boots. Caroline tells him that they are black. Raymond confesses that he was in debt before the murder, so he has a motive. Poirot tells Sheppard that he suspects Parker and gets Parker to recreate his actions that night. From this, Poirot works out that Flora never saw Roger on the night of his death. She stole the £40 and pretended to be leaving the study when she saw Parker. However, Blunt offers to take the blame for her and Poirot tells him to confess his love for her. Parker reveals that he blackmailed his previous boss and was trying to eavesdrop on Roger but had not learnt anything from it.

A man, Charles Kent, is arrested in Liverpool, suspected of being the strange visitor. Poirot and Sheppard go to meet him. It turns out that he is the illegitimate son of Miss Russell, who met him in the summerhouse. He is a cocaine addict who wanted money off his mother, who asked Sheppard about drug use as well as poisons.

ALL IS REVEALED

Poirot confronts Ursula, who is revealed to be Ralph's wife. She threw her wedding ring in the pond after Ralph decided to marry Flora to secure his inheritance. Ursula had told Roger the truth, which led to her being sacked and caused Roger to threaten to disinherit Ralph, giving Ralph a strong motive to murder him before he could change his will.

Poirot gathers the suspects and reveals that Roger had recently bought a dictaphone, which was what Raymond heard. Poirot brings Ralph into the room, revealing that Sheppard had been hiding him to protect him. Poirot tells the room that he knows who the murderer is and that they should come forward to protect the innocent Ralph.

Poirot then discusses the case alone with Sheppard. Poirot reveals that the phone call, which had puzzled him from the beginning, allowed the killer to remove the dictaphone from the study and accuses Sheppard himself. Poirot explains that Sheppard must have set the dictaphone to play a recording of Roger at half past nine, tricking Raymond into thinking he was alive when Sheppard had murdered him earlier. The fake phone call ensured that Sheppard was the first to discover the body, allowing him to quickly remove the dictaphone. Sheppard then framed Ralph while pretending to protect him.

Poirot accuses Sheppard of being the blackmailer, having realised that Mr Ferrars was poisoned when examining the body. Poirot gives Sheppard the opportunity to commit suicide to protect his reputation and therefore spare Caroline from the truth. Sheppard writes his confession and takes an overdose.

CHARACTER STUDY

DR JAMES SHEPPARD

Sheppard, the narrator of the novel, is a doctor with a keen interest in mechanical devices and appears to be a reliable, friendly man. Poirot seems to like him and compares him to his faithful companion Captain Hastings, who frequently narrates Poirot novels. We are naturally disposed to trust the narrator of a tale, so we do not suspect him of the murder, making the revelation of his crimes all the more shocking. The novel's ending makes it clear that Sheppard is a weak man, whose desperation to solve his financial difficulties led him to commit terrible acts.

Despite him being the narrator, we learn very little about Sheppard. However, there are some indications that he is not as nice as we initially assume. His descriptions of other characters tend to be negative and he looks down on the residents of King's Abbot. This arrogance contrasts with his outwardly pleasant manner. He does not appear to feel remorse when his crimes are discovered, and willingly murdered his close friend Roger, suggesting that he can be cold and detached.

HERCULE POIROT

Poirot is Christie's most famous creation: a Belgian detective whose arrogance sometimes annoys those around him. At the beginning of the novel, Poirot has retired. His friend, Roger, has agreed to help him remain anonymous in town, going by the name of 'Mr Porrot'. Despite having what others view as unusual habits, Poirot is a brilliant detective, using his psychological assessments of his suspects to deduce a motive for the crime. Poirot is not motivated by a desire for fame or fortune; he simply wants to find the answer to the puzzle and says that he cannot stop once he has begun an investigation. His decision to let Sheppard commit suicide demonstrates that legal justice is not his main priority.

Poirot often uses French words instead of their English alternatives, highlighting his outsider status in King's Abbot, which is every inch a traditional English town. Sheppard describes Poirot as "little" with an "egg-shaped head" and "two immense moustaches" (p. 21).

ROGER ACKROYD

The titular Roger Ackroyd is, not surprisingly, the murder victim and his death is the catalyst for the events of the novel. Ackroyd is a wealthy manufacturer of around 50, who Sheppard says resembles the stereotype of a country squire. His wife (an alcoholic) died many years before the start of the novel and he has recently become involved with Mrs Ferrars. We are told that he is well-liked in the village, but his family claim that he was mean with his money and it is revealed that there was a lot of tension in his household prior to his death.

CAROLINE SHEPPARD

Caroline is Sheppard's sister, with whom he resides. She is incredibly nosy and loves to gossip, so the case fascinates her. Sheppard is baffled by her ability to find out so much despite staying in the house. Her misguided attempts to investigate provide much of the novel's humour, though she makes several accurate observations. For example, she guesses that Mrs Ferrars murdered her husband. Although Sheppard looks down on his sister, comparing her to an "mongoose rampant"

(p. 7), he appears to care deeply for her and ultimately commits suicide to spare her the shame of his crimes being revealed. Christie liked the character of Caroline and later stated that she was the inspiration for the character of Miss Marple.

FLORA ACKROYD

Flora is Roger's young niece, who has lived with him since the death of her father. Flora is beautiful and charming, though Sheppard states "quite a lot of people do not like Flora Ackroyd" (p. 31). She is engaged to Ralph, to whom she is intensely loyal, though she does not seem to love him. Flora resents her dependency on Roger for money and stole money from his desk on the night of the murder. She is, however, upset by his death and it is Flora who requests that Poirot investigate. The murder gives Flora financial independence and she chooses to marry Hector Blunt.

MRS ACKROYD

Flora's mother, Mrs Ackroyd, is also financially dependent on Roger and has many debts. She moved into Roger's house after the death of her husband, Roger's "ne'er-do-well younger brother"

(p. 14). On the day of Roger's death, she searched his office for his will. Sheppard dislikes her, describing her as "coldly speculative" (p. 32).

RALPH PATON

Ralph is Roger's stepson, who is described as handsome and charming, though weak-willed. He is initially the main suspect in the murder: he frequently argued with Roger over money and disappeared straight after the murder. Ralph is engaged to Flora but is revealed to already be married to Ursula Bourne. When Roger found this out, he threatened to disown him, giving Ralph a financial motive for the murder. However, it is revealed that he was set up by Dr Sheppard, who had hidden him away while pretending to be his friend.

URSULA BOURNE

Ursula is a maid in Roger's house who was sacked on the morning of the murder and has no alibi. She was born to an upper-class family but had to take a job to support herself. She later admits that she is married to Ralph and became frustrated with his plan to marry Flora to sort out his finances. She told Roger the truth, causing him to sack her.

GEOFFREY RAYMOND

Raymond is Roger's efficient and hard-working secretary. He confesses to Poirot that he was in debt before the murder, but that his inheritance has helped him. Raymond makes a positive impression on Poirot and Sheppard.

MAJOR HECTOR BLUNT

Blunt is a close friend of Roger and has a reputation for his hunting exploits. He is a straightforward man and is never truly a suspect in the murder: the only thing he is concealing is his love for Flora. He is not good with words but shows his devotion to her by taking responsibility for her theft. Flora accepts his proposal when the truth about Ralph is revealed.

PARKER

Parker is Roger's butler and has a habit of eavesdropping. Sheppard says he has a "fat, smug, oily face" and there is "something decidedly shifty in his eye" (p. 41). His suspicious nature causes him to become a chief suspect in the case and Poirot believes him to be the blackmailer for a while.

He eventually confesses that he did blackmail his previous employer and was unsuccessfully trying to find out Roger's secret.

MISS RUSSELL

Miss Russell is Roger's housekeeper. It is suggested by Sheppard that she wished to marry Roger prior to his relationship with Mrs Ferrars. She has "pinched lips" and "an acid smile" (p. 14). She comes under suspicion after asking Sheppard for information about drugs, but it is later revealed that she was concerned about her drug-addicted, illegitimate son. She met with him on the night of the murder to give him money. Her reputation is of the utmost importance to her, leading to her refusing to publicly acknowledge her child.

ANALYSIS

THE DETECTIVE NOVEL

Detective novels are in many ways a game between the reader and the author, in which the reader is challenged to decipher the clues and identify the murderer before the detective does. As a genre, detective tales tend to be highly formulaic. This is especially true of Christie's novels, which all follow a very similar pattern. Traits common to detective novels include:

- a murder;
- a collection of suspects who all have motive and opportunity;
- an unusually intelligent detective who can spot clues most would miss;
- a sidekick narrator who the audience can relate to;
- a concluding summation in which the detective explains his findings.

Christie uses all these features in *The Murder of Roger Ackroyd*, but plays with many of them to keep the reader on their toes:

- Evidently Roger Ackroyd is murdered, which triggers Poirot's investigation. The mysterious nature of his death fits with the tropes of detective fiction, but this is not the only murder in the novel. Mr Ferrars is murdered by his wife a year prior to the beginning of the novel. This murder went undetected and was not investigated, which is highly unusual for a novel of this kind.

- Christie follows the second convention. There are numerous suspects in Ackroyd's murder, all of whom have a motive. The motives are mainly financial and the reader struggles to discount any of them from the investigation. As Poirot says to the group: "Every one of you in this room is concealing something" (p. 124).

- Poirot is a clear example of a traditional fictional detective. He is highly intelligent and solves crimes that baffle both the police and the reader. However, like his fellow fictional detective Sherlock Holmes, he can be abrasive. His nationality makes him stand out as different to those around him and his reputation damages the pride of the police officers. Like many fictional detectives,

Poirot is not an official police officer; he solves puzzles for enjoyment.

- It would not be very interesting to read a detective novel narrated by the detective, as the reader would see the exact same clues as him, removing much of the mystery. Therefore, a likeable narrator of average intellect is needed to tell the story. In Poirot novels, this role is often filled by Captain Hastings. Poirot describes "his naivete, his honest outlook, the pleasure of delighting and surprising him by my superior gifts" (p. 22) to Sheppard and suggests that Sheppard take on a similar role. Of course, as discussed below, Sheppard proves to be a great subversion of this trope, as he is in fact the murderer.

- Christie herself popularised the idea of a concluding summation and there is a very clear example at the end of the novel. Poirot gathers all the main suspects together and talks them through his findings, revealing Ralph's location. However, Poirot subverts expectations by not revealing the murderer's identity to the group; he instead confronts Sheppard alone.

WATSON THE MURDERER

Christie shocked the literary establishment when she revealed that Roger Ackroyd was murdered by the narrator, James Sheppard. She was accused of breaking the rules of detective fiction and deceiving the reader. But isn't the point of detective fiction to attempt to trick the reader? What made this twist so shocking?

Arthur Conan Doyle popularised the idea of a detective's sidekick when he created Dr John Watson, roughly half a century before *The Murder of Roger Ackroyd* was written. Watson is reliable, funny and very honest, often playing the straight man to the more unconventional character of Sherlock Holmes. He is the person that the reader should identify with, a normal man observing a genius at work. As stated, Christie created a similar character in Poirot's loyal friend Hastings. The most emphasised feature of these narrators is their trustworthy nature, which is why the reader would never think to suspect them. Sheppard bears many similarities to these men. He is a doctor, so is expected to preserve life and is respected by the community. He attempts to maintain his clients' confidentiality, which makes him appear trustworthy, and he appears keen to help Poirot. His dislike of other people's traits, such as Caroline's gossiping ways, indicates that he is above these flaws himself.

However, all of this is a cover for Sheppard's true nature. Of course, Christie does drop hints to the murderer's identity throughout the novel. Sheppard never lies in his narration, though he does conceal his misdeeds. For example, he never explicitly states that the phone call was to say Ackroyd had been murdered. He simply tells us that that is what he tells Caroline. On seeing the body, he does "what little had to be done" (p. 45). He was hiding the dictaphone in his bag, but the reader assumes he is examining the body as a doctor should. The reader's absolute trust in the narrator means that these clues remain unseen.

UNAVOIDABLE EVIL

The revelation of Sheppard as the murderer confirms one of the main themes of the novel: nobody can be trusted. Practically every character in the text comes under suspicion and almost everybody is hiding something. Poirot does not dismiss anybody based on appearance or even personality: he believes that anybody could be the murderer in the right circumstances.

King's Abbot is presented in the novel as a normal, sleepy, English village. Roger Ackroyd, a "country squire", is "the life and soul of [the] peaceful village of King's Abbot" (p. 12). This emphasises the traditional nature of the village, which revolves around a stereotypical squire. Sheppard even says it is "very much like any other village" (*ibid*.). However, Roger only appears to be a squire. He is an industrialist, suggesting that all is not as it seems in the village. In fact, resentment and secrets lurk below the surface of everyday life. Even characters who appear innocent, such as the young, pretty Flora, are concealing things. Flora is a particularly striking example, as Sheppard describes her as "a simple straightforward English girl" (p. 31). If she can have secrets, so could all English girls, and by extension all of society. Respectable figures, such as Parker the butler, are revealed to have committed crimes in the past. And if this is true of King's Abbot, a typical village, it must be true of everywhere.

Of course, this secrecy is necessary for a detective novel. However, Christie's analysis of her villain's character is quite unusual. She does not dismiss him as a purely one-dimensional, evil villain and acknowledges the role of both nature and nurture in his development. This is shown in Poirot's lengthy description of the murderer to Sheppard in Chapter 17: "Let us take a man – a very ordinary man. A man with no idea of murder in his heart. There is in him somewhere a strain of weakness – deep down. It has so far never been called into play. Perhaps it never will be – and if so he will go to his grave honoured and respected by everyone" (p. 168). This suggests that many people could be driven to murder in the right circumstances, especially as most characters demonstrate a degree of weakness in the novel. Evil seems unavoidable in a society as secretive and corrupt as this one.

FURTHER REFLECTION

SOME QUESTIONS TO THINK ABOUT...

- Did you predict the novel's twist ending? Did you enjoy the twist, or do you feel it was too unexpected?
- At the end of the novel, Poirot allows Sheppard to commit suicide rather than be arrested. Do you agree with this form of justice?
- The characters are all hiding things of varying importance to the case. Can you relate to any of their dilemmas? Are some of the concealments worse than others or are all equally immoral for not being honest with Poirot?
- How do you interpret Sheppard's relationship with Caroline? Did your opinion change through the novel?
- On rereading the novel, can you spot any clues to the murderer's identity that you missed the first time around?
- How does class impact on the behaviour of the characters in the novel? Does social standing play a large part in the mystery?

- Compare Poirot's approach to the investigation to that of the police. How does Christie highlight the differences between Poirot and Inspector Raglan? Are there any similarities between them?
- Poirot's use of logic is greatly praised in the novel. However, Caroline comes to several accurate conclusions about the case using intuition and her network of gossip, and Poirot even asks her to aid him at times. What does this suggest about her character and about investigative techniques?
- Christie has previously been criticised for focusing on plot at the expense of characterisation, with many of her characters being two-dimensional. Do you think this is a fair criticism? How important is characterisation when writing detective fiction?

We want to hear from you!
Leave a comment on your online library
and share your favourite books on social media!

FURTHER READING

REFERENCE EDITION

- Christie, A. (1957) *The Murder of Roger Ackroyd*. London: Fontana.

REFERENCE STUDIES

- Agatha Christie Ltd. (2016) *90 Years of Christie Favourite: The Murder of Roger Ackroyd*. [Online]. [Accessed 14 January 2019]. Available from: <https://www.agathachristie.com/news/2016/90-years-of-christie-favourite-the-murder-of-roger-ackroyd>
- Madison Davis, J. (2015) Playing by the Rules. *World Literature Today*. 89, (3-4), pp. 29-31.

ADDITIONAL SOURCES

- Christie, A. (1977) *Agatha Christie: An Autobiography*. London: Collins.

ADAPTATIONS

- *Alibi* by Michael Morton. (1928) [Play]. Gerald Du Maurier. Dir. Prince of Wales Theatre.

- *Alibi.* (1931) [Film]. Leslie S. Hiscott. Dir. UK: Julius Hagen Productions.

- *Agatha Christie's Poirot: The Murder of Roger Ackroyd.* (2000) [Television show]. Andrew Grieve. Dir. UK, USA: Carnival Film & Television, A&E Television Networks, Agatha Christie Ltd, British Broadcasting Corporation, Picture Partnership Productions.

MORE FROM BRIGHTSUMMARIES.COM

- Reading guide – *And Then There Were None* by Agatha Christie.

Bright ≡Summaries.com

BOOK ANALYSIS

More guides to rediscover your love of literature

Animal Farm
BY GEORGE ORWELL

The Stranger
BY ALBERT CAMUS

Harry Potter and the Sorcerer's Stone
BY J.K. ROWLING

The Silence of the Sea
BY VERCORS

Antigone
BY JEAN ANOUILH

The Flowers of Evil
BY BAUDELAIRE

www.brightsummaries.com

Although the editor makes every effort to
verify the accuracy of the information published,
BrightSummaries.com accepts no responsibility for
the content of this book.

© BrightSummaries.com, 2019. All rights reserved.

www.brightsummaries.com

Ebook EAN: 9782808017206

Paperback EAN: 9782808017213

Legal Deposit: D/2019/12603/27

Cover: © Primento

Digital conception by Primento, the digital partner of
publishers.

Printed in Great Britain
by Amazon

36510686R10029